PARTY FOR TWO

WAYS TO ADD
LOVE AND LAUGHTER
TO YOUR RELATIONSHIP

BY

Joyce L. Karchmar

authorHOUSE®

AuthorHouse™
1663 Liberty Drive
Bloomington, IN 47403
www.authorhouse.com
Phone: 1-800-839-8640

Published by AuthorHouse 01/31/2015

ISBN: 978-1-4343-2911-0 (sc)

Library of Congress Control Number: 2007906945

Printed in the United States of America
Bloomington, Indiana

To my HONEY –

who added so much

"LOVE and LAUGHTER"

to my life, I thank you.

You are my inspiration.

INTRODUCTION

"Don't look for a lover" - companion or playmate. "Be one." - to paraphrase the late novelist James Leo Herlihy.

Whenever you make someone feel special, you show them love. You can be playful, cute, loving or sexy. You can start traditions and create yearly anticipation about what's going to happen. The best idea of all – is the one that brings a smile or laughter to the one you love. Humor enhances intimacy and elevates the soul.

There are many occasions to celebrate in life – not just birthdays, anniversaries and major holidays. It only takes one idea to make a single day different than the rest.

On the following pages, you'll find suggestions for special occasions and holidays. The lists are not all inclusive, you can probably think of more. However, I think this will put you on the right track.

All of the following ideas may not be suitable for everyone, but surely you can find at least one suggestion that will add "more love and laughter" to your relationship.

CONTENTS

EPILOGUE

TIMES FOR LOVE AND LAUGHTER

ANYTIME

You can express your loving, playful, sexy side anytime. You don't need a special occasion. Just do whatever it takes to make your loved one smile or laugh. Try some of these ideas:

ANYTIME

1-   Give a CARD: place it in the refrigerator, in the microwave, in a drawer, in a kitchen cabinet, under a pillow or in a toolbox - anywhere you know it will be found

2-   Leave suggestive MESSAGES or play appropriate songs on your Honey's voice mail - only if the voice mail is private

3-   For MEN: just once, wear only a necktie - or a necktie and underwear, around the house or apartment

4-   For WOMEN: wear only a matching bra and panties set, wear only panties, or wear only silk boxer shorts - his or yours, around the house or apartment

5-   Invite your Honey to join you in the BATHTUB or SHOWER for some cleanly togetherness

6-   Leave a TRAIL OF CLOTHES on the floor - leading to you

7-   On a rainy day or night, STRIP DOWN to your underwear - or nothing, and run outside onto the deck or in the yard together

8-   Use a CHEF'S HAT when cooking inside or grilling outside

♥

9- Take your clothes off, hide and leave sticky-note CLUES for your Partner to find you

10- Offer a MASSAGE with baby oil or scented oil

11- Wear only an APRON when cooking or serving food

12- Write ENDEARING WORDS on shells, stones, pieces of sticky paper or even toilet paper, and place them around the house, apartment or in the car – anywhere they will be found

13- Buy PLASTIC HANDCUFFS

14- Make love in EVERY ROOM of the apartment or house at least once - even the stairs

15- Have your Honey find you dressed in a FUNNY OUTFIT

16- Hug and kiss, or more in a PARKED CAR - regardless of your age

17- Greet your Sweetie at the door with NOTHING on

18- Place a small gift under the BED PILLOW

19- Write a message on your body using WASHABLE MARKERS

20- Make the WORLD your BEDROOM - without getting arrested

♥

SPECIAL OCCASIONS

JOB/ BUSINESS

When someone you care about starts a new job, is promoted or gets a sought after account, it's a time to make them feel special. There are several ways to celebrate the accomplishment:

NEW JOB
PROMOTION/ BONUS/ RAISE
ACQUIRING THE BIG ACCOUNT

1-   Model silk boxers with DOLLAR SIGN design – man or woman

2-   Place a CONGRATULATIONS card in the kitchen, bathroom or bedroom

3-   Make love in a new place or in a new way – to CELEBRATE

4-   Serve a special CELEBRATION breakfast, lunch, dinner or dessert

5-   Play or sing *WE'RE IN THE MONEY, GOT A JOB, PENNIES FROM HEAVEN or MONEY MAKES THE WORLD GO ROUND* and dance together

6-   Wear a MONEY theme apron with almost nothing (or nothing) underneath – man or woman

7-   Use DOLLAR SIGN or CONGRATULATIONS stickers on your face or body for your Honey to discover

8-   Prepare DOLLAR SIGN shaped pasta

9-   Leave a trail of paper DOLLARS or COINS - leading to you

♥

10-   Entice your Sweetie to search for PLAY MONEY hidden in your clothes

11-   Hang CONGRATULATIONS banners around the apartment or the house

12-   Use DOLLAR SIGN print toilet paper

13-   Share a bottle of CHAMPAGNE, WINE or the Honoree's favorite BEVERAGE

14-   Give a t-shirt with CONGRATULATIONS on the front or back

15-   Draw DOLLAR SIGNS on your body for your Partner to discover - use washable markers

16-   Sleep on pillowcases with COINS or DOLLAR SIGN print

17-   Surprise the Honoree with a DOLLAR SIGN shaped chocolate bar, a $100,000 or PAY DAY candy bar

18-   Find a CONTRATULATIONS or DOLLAR SIGN theme mug

19-   Be a SERVANT-FOR-THE-DAY OR NIGHT - fulfilling your Honey's wishes

♥

MEDICAL

Whenever someone is sick or needs medical attention, it can be scary. If you can show that person love and bring a smile to his or her face, it's the best medicine you can give them. Consider these ideas to make that special someone feel better:

COLD OR FLU
RETURN HOME FROM
<u>MEDICAL PROCEDURE / HOSPITAL</u>

1-   Dress as a DOCTOR or a NURSE – wear white

2-   Use a toy STETHOSCOPE to listen your Honey's heartbeat

3-   Write "GET WELL" somewhere on your body where it will be seen - use washable markers

4-   Wear RUBBER GLOVES

5-   Hang WELCOME HOME banners where they can be seen, when your Sweetie returns from the hospital

6-   Plant lots of KISSES wherever it hurts

7-   Serve PUDDING or JELL-O and eat it off of the Patient's belly

8-   Make a BLOODY MARY cocktail with or without liquor – claiming blood count may be low

9-   Give or send a suggestive or funny CARD

♥

10-   Wear STICKERS or BANDAGES on your face or body to make the Patient laugh

11-   Buy favorite FOODS, JUICES or MAGAZINES for your Honey

12-   Serve breakfast in BED

13-   Place GLOW-IN-THE-DARK STARS on the ceiling or walls, so the Patient can see the stars without leaving the bed

14-   Prepare soup with CHICKEN shaped pasta

15-   Rent his or her favorite MOVIES to watch together

16-   Offer to RUB your Honey's shoulders, back or feet

17-   Give CANDY PILLS (jelly beans) as a prescription to feel better

18-   Add champagne to the ORANGE JUICE

19-   Lie next to the Patient until he or she FALLS ASLEEP

♥

NATURE

Nature creates many wonderful occurrences. The following suggestions will help you enjoy some of these special times:

FULL MOON
ECLIPSE OF THE MOON

1-   Give a t-shirt or nightshirt with a SOLAR SYSTEM theme

2-   Place STAR or MOON stickers on your face or body for your Honey to discover

3-   Suggest making love outside under the MOON or during the ECLIPSE - weather permitting

4-   Buy MOON or STARS print silk boxers - for man or woman

5-   Use pillowcases with a MOON or SOLAR SYSTEM theme

6-   Together – strip down to underwear - or nothing, and view the MOON or ECLIPSE on the deck or in the back yard

7-   Wear MOON or STARS theme underwear for your Partner to discover

8-   MOON him or her

9-   Serve STAR - shaped pasta

10-   Walk under the FULL MOON with your Honey

♥

1ST SNOWFALL
ANY SNOWFALL

1- Model a WHITE apron with little or nothing underneath – man or woman

2- TOGETHER – strip down to underwear or nothing, and run outside onto the deck or in the back yard

3- Serve hot chocolate or coffee, and spice it with PEPPERMINT SCHNAPPS or BAILEYS

4- Have a SNOWBALL FIGHT – then kiss and make up

5- Make love in front of a ROARING FIRE

6- Take a walk together when the SNOW is falling

7- Buy WHITE silk boxers, WHITE robe or WHITE pajamas – for man or woman

8- Use SNOWFLAKE stickers on your face or body for your Honey to discover

9- Wear EARMUFFS to bed - remove after the laughter stops

10- Hide paper SNOWFLAKES or SNOWMEN in your clothes and have your Sweetie search for them

♥

PERSONAL

Whatever the occasion, celebrate for one week rather than one day. Do something special every morning or night that week - eat out, give small presents or cards, meet for lunch, have wine with dinner each night, or any combination of things. Whatever you do should make the week special for your Honey. You can use different types of candles for cakes, cupcakes, muffins, donuts, toast, meatloaf, mashed potatoes, etc. Be creative. There is a large variety of candles to choose from: chili peppers, teddy bears, champagne bottles, telephones, golf clubs, golf balls, footballs, basketballs, chocolate bars, beer cans, construction cones, cars, wrapped presents, dynamite sticks, tools, etc.

BIRTHDAYS
ANNIVERSARIES

Celebrate your Honey's BIRTHDAY WEEK, or your ANNIVERSARY WEEK. Here are suggestions for ANNIVERSARY DATES you can celebrate:

1ST Meeting

1ST Date

Engagement or college-pin date

Date became intimate

Date moved in together

Marriage date

Date purchased condo or house

The list is virtually endless!

♥

NEW CAR

1-   Surprise your Honey with a small GIFT for the
       inside of the new car

2-   Take a picture of the NEW CAR with the Proud
       Owner in it or next to it

3-   Buy a TOY MODEL of the new car and run it up and
       down your Sweetie's body

4-   Suggest hugging, kissing or more in the NEW CAR
       – to CELBRATE

5-   Together – decide on a name for the NEW CAR
       using a name based on the first letter of the make or
       model, ex – Abby Acura, Nicky Nissan, Jenny Jeep,
       Courtney Corolla or Eddie Explorer

6-   Wear or buy a t-shirt with NEW CAR name or
       picture on front or back

7-   Give the Proud Owner AUTOMOBILE print silk
       boxers

8-   Find a matching color BLANKET for the two of you to
       use in or on top of the car

9-   Send or give a NEW CAR card

10-   Place AUTOMOBILE stickers on your face or body
       for your Honey to discover

♥

SPECIAL RECOGNITION
ELECTION/ APPOINTMENT
COLLEGE DEGREE OR LICENSE

1-   Serve a SPECIAL RECOGNITION breakfast, lunch, dinner or dessert to your Honey

2-   Model or give silk boxers with a SPECIAL RECOGNITION theme

3-   Make love in a special place or in a special way – to CELEBRATE

4-   Leave a small GIFT or CARD under your Sweetie's pillow

5-   Wear a GRADUATION CAP or other appropriate HAT to bed - remove when fun begins

6-   Buy a frame to display the AWARD, DEGREE or LICENSE

7-   Use DIPLOMA or TROPHY stickers on your face or body for the Honoree to discover

8-   Write CONGRATULATIONS on stones or sticky papers – place them in cabinets, pockets or shoes

9-   Give a SPECIAL RECOGNITION t-shirt or nightshirt – man or woman

10-   Hang CONGRATULATIONS banners

♥

SPORTS

If you or your Honey like Football, Baseball or other sports, the following ideas will surely get a laugh or a smile:

SUPERBOWL
COLLEGE BOWL GAMES

1-   Prepare FOOTBALL shaped pasta

2-   Wear a FOOTBALL theme t-shirt, nightshirt or silk
      boxers

3-   Place FOOTBALL stickers on your face or body for
      your Honey to discover

4-   Serve a special FOOTBALL breakfast, lunch, dinner,
      or dessert – to have this day every year

5-   Use a TOY FOOTBALL to toss and/or tackle your
      Sweetie during commercials

6-   Write "TOUCHDOWN" on your body where it can be
      discovered – use washable markers

7-   Give your Partner colorful ELBOW or KNEE PADS

8-   Serve candy or nuts in a new ATHLETIC CUP

9-   Surprise your Honey with TICKETS to the game

10-   Buy FOOTBALL theme toilet paper

♥

OPENING DAY OF BASEBALL

1-   Wear a BASEBALL CAP to bed - remove when laughter stops

2-   Serve a special BASEBALL breakfast, lunch, dinner or dessert - to have this day every year

3-   Use BASEBALL theme or team logo pillowcases

4-   Greet your Honey wearing BASEBALL print boxers

5-   Buy chocolate candy in BASEBALL wrappers

6-   Place BASEBALL stickers on your face or body for your Partner to discover

7-   Model a BASEBALL/ team logo t-shirt or nightshirt at breakfast or to watch the game

8-   Write "HOME RUN" on your body where it can be discovered - use washable markers

9-   Hide a BASEBALL under the pillow or between the sheets for your Sweetie to find

10-   Surprise your Honey with TICKETS to the game

♥

KENTUCKY DERBY

1-   Serve MINT JULEP cocktails

2-   Use HORSE stickers on your face or body for your Honey to discover

3-   Model a large FANCY HAT or a TOP HAT with underwear or with nothing else

4-   Give HORSE RACING theme silk boxers - to him or her

5-   Prepare a special KENTUCKY DERBY breakfast, lunch, dinner or dessert – to have this day every year

6-   Sleep on HORSE theme pillowcases

7-   Choose your favorite horse and make a SUGGESTIVE BET on which horse will win

8-   Wear a HORSE RACING t-shirt or nightshirt to breakfast or to watch the race

9-   Surprise your Sweetie with tickets to the KENTUCKY DERBY

10-   Buy a mug with KENTUCKY DERBY or HORSE theme

♥

DAYTONA 500
INDIANAPOLIS 500

1-   Buy a TOY RACE CAR to run up and down your
       Honey's body

2-   Place RACE CAR stickers on your face or body for
       your Sweetie to discover

3-   Serve a special RACE CAR breakfast, lunch, dinner
       or dessert - to have this day every year

4-   Wear RACE CAR   print silk boxers

5-   Surprise your Partner with a soft TOY RACE CAR
       under the bed pillow

6-   Choose your favorite driver and make a
       SUGGESTIVE BET on who will win

7-   Use RACE CAR pillowcases on the bed

8-   Find a RACE CAR shaped sponge for bathing or
       showering together

9-   Wave a CHECKERED FLAG when you want your
       Honey to come to bed

10-   Give a RACE CAR pillow to use while watching the
       race

♥

FISHING SEASON

1-   Model HIP BOOTS or a FISHING HAT with nothing else on

2-   Serve a special FISH lunch or dinner

3-   Buy your Honey a FISH shaped pillow

4-   Surprise your Sweetie with a TOY FISH under the pillow

5-   Write "HOOKED ON YOU" on your body where it can be found – use washable markers

6-   Give FISH print silk boxers to him or her

7-   Place FISH stickers on your face or body for your Honey to discover

8-   Wear a FISH HAT or a FISHING HAT to bed - remove when the laughter stops

9-   Use a FISH shaped sponge when you bathe or shower together

10-   Model a t-shirt or nightshirt imprinted with "HOOKED ON YOU"

♥

TRAVEL

When someone you love, or both of you, will be traveling by plane, boat or train – there are many ways to make the occasion memorable. Consider these ideas:

AIRPLANE FLIGHT

1-   Write suggestive "AIRPLANE" words or phrases on the beverage napkin

2-   Leave the lavatory with your UNDERWEAR in your pocket – part of it showing

3-   Give a funny or suggestive gift associated with FLYING or the DESTINATION

4-   Suggest joining the MILE HIGH club

5-   Speak to pilot or steward to get a set of WINGS for your Honey

6-   Request a BLANKET to put over both of you - to hide your hands

7-   Return to your seat WEARING funny glasses, fake mustache or stickers on your face

8-   Buy AIRPLANE theme silk boxers for him or her

9-   Tell your Sweetie to guess where you have AIRPLANE stickers on your body

♥

CRUISE

1-   Wear a CAPTAIN'S HAT to bed – remove when the laughter stops

2-   Place a funny GIFT or a CARD in her cosmetic case, his toiletry case, or dresser drawer

3-   Tell waiter that it is your Honey's BIRTHDAY whether it is or not – the waiter will usually bring a small cake to the table and sing

4-   Model CRUISE theme silk boxers with nothing else on, in your cabin

5-   Find at least one SECLUDED spot on the ship to hug, kiss or more

6-   Make love in a different way to celebrate your LAST NIGHT on board the ship

7-   Buy a small toy BOAT to place under the pillow before bedtime

8-   Use SHIP stickers on your face or body for your Honey to discover

9-   Play or sing *NIGHT CRUISE, SEA CRUISE, SAILING* or *LOVE BOAT* and dance together in your room

♥

TRAIN RIDE

1-   Have your Honey guess where you have placed
      TRAIN stickers on your body

2-   Leave the lavatory with your UNDERWEAR in your
      pocket - part of it showing

3-   Buy TRAIN print silk boxers for him or her

4-   Find a funny or suggestive gift associated with a
      TRAIN RIDE or your DESTINATION

5-   Suggest your Honey join you in the LAVATORY for
      a hug, kiss or more

6-   Return to your seat WEARING funny glasses, a
      mustache, or stickers on your face

7-   Give a funny or a romantic card with a picture of a
      TRAIN on the front

8-   Write suggestive TRAIN related words or phrases
      and give them to your Honey

9-   Request a BLANKET to put over both of you - to hide
      your hands

♥

LEAVE / RETURN FROM TRIP

1-   Buy a card or small gift to HIDE in your Honey's suitcase or travel bag

2-   Place several funny or loving NOTES in pockets, in shoes and between packed clothes

3-   Find a CD of your Partner's favorite songs to enjoy during the trip

4-   Secretly PACK silk boxers – for him or her

5-   Give a special CARE PACKAGE of things to use while away

6-   Pick up your Sweetie at the airport or train station WEARING funny glasses, a fake mustache, stickers on your face or a funny hat

7-   Stick funny or loving NOTES in the apartment or house, for your Honey to find - when you are away

8-   Leave funny or suggestive MESSAGES on your Partner's private voice mail

9-   Hang WELCOME HOME banners around the apartment or house

♥

WHILE IN HOTEL / MOTEL

1-   Leave the bathroom WEARING funny glasses, a fake mustache, his or her underwear - where ever it fits, or stickers on your face

2-   Hide a CARD in the dresser drawer or under the pillow - for your Honey to find

3-   Wear a CAP or HAT to bed - appropriate for the location or season, and remove when the laughter stops

4-   Place funny or suggestive NOTES or PHRASES in his or her pockets or shoes

5-   SHOWER or BATHE together

6-   Model special UNDERWEAR - man or woman

7-   Make a GOODIES PACKAGE of your Partner's favorite treats

8-   Buy a small STUFFED ANIMAL to put under your Honey's pillow during this trip and for future trips

9-   Play or sing your special LOVE SONGS and dance together

♥

SEASONS OF LOVE AND LAUGHTER

SPRING

The "1st DAY OF SPRING" is a time when nature starts to come alive again. Thoughts turn to love – and of course to other things, including flowers, gardening and planning more outdoor activities. There are several ways to make this day special:

1ST DAY OF SPRING - MARCH

ACTIVITIES

1-   Dress up as a doctor or a nurse – to help with
      SPRING FEVER

2-   Place FLOWER stickers on your face or on your
      body where only your Honey will discover them

3-   Play or sing *YOU GIVE ME FEVER* and dance
      together

4-   Wear a SPRING bonnet or BASEBALL cap to bed
      - remove when the laughter stops

5-   Make love OUTSIDE in a sleeping bag or on a
      blanket – in the yard or on the deck

6-   Entice your Partner to play doctor and examine you
      because you have SPRING FEVER

7-   Make the bed with YELLOW, LAVENDER or
      FLOWER print sheets and pillowcases

8-   Use FRUIT or FLOWER shaped sponge for
      showering or bathing together

9-   Share a list of fun things to do outside this SPRING
      with your Honey

10-   Greet your Sweetie at the door – wearing nothing but
      the FLOWER in your hand

GIFTS

1-   FLOWER seeds, small plant, yard gloves, magazine or candy - in a clay pot

2-   Mug with FLOWER or SPRING FEVER theme

3-   BRIGHT color underwear for him/ BRIGHT color undies or teddy for her

4-   Bird house for the LOVE BIRDS

5-   Thermometer to check for SPRING FEVER

FOOD

1-   Serve a special SPRING breakfast, lunch, dinner or dessert

2-   Drink coffee or tea OUTSIDE - on the patio or the deck

3-   Prepare BUNNY shaped pasta

4-   Plan an indoor PICNIC - eat on the floor or on the bed

5-   Arrange a platter of cheeses, crackers and FRUIT

♥

SUMMER

The "1st DAY OF SUMMER" is a time of fun and sharing activities outside, as the weather turns warmer. Try these special ideas:

1st DAY OF SUMMER - JUNE

ACTIVITIES

1-   Share a list of FUN things you would like to do outside with your Honey this SUMMER - maybe skinny dipping

2-   Buy a WATERMELON shaped sponge for the kitchen or for showering together

3-   Wear SUNGLASSES or SUNVISOR to bed - remove when laughter stops

4-   Write suggestive or funny phrases on STONES or SHELLS; leave them around where he or she can see them, or put them in drawers, shoes or pockets

5-   Place SUMMER theme stickers on your body for your Sweetie to discover

6-   Play or sing *SUMMERTIME* or *HERE COMES SUMMER*, or other SUMMER songs and dance together

7-   SUNBATHE together in the nude – on the deck, in the yard or at a private beach

8-   Wear a CHEF'S HAT when grilling

9-   Rub ICE CUBES on your Honey

10-   Make love OUTSIDE at night

GIFTS

1-   Water squirt-gun, hiking sox, sand toys or funny
       sunglasses - in a PAIL

2-   Book or magazine featuring SUMMER ideas –
       grilling, gardening, or beaches

3-   Silk boxers with SUMMER or FRUIT theme for your
       Honey – man or woman

4-   FRUIT or SUMMER theme apron

5-   Underwear in bright SUMMER colors for him/ undies
       or teddy in bright SUMMER colors for her

FOOD

1-   Prepare PALM TREE, FLAMINGO, SAILBOAT or
       LOBSTER shaped pasta

2-   Enjoy at least one meal, coffee or cocktail OUTSIDE
       on this day every year

3-   Serve your Sweetie's favorite ICE CREAM

4-   Cook on the GRILL and eat OUTSIDE, or eat in the
       car or on the bed if it rains

5-   Share a big, juicy WATERMELON with your Honey

FALL

The "1ST DAY OF FALL" makes you think of indoor activities as the weather grows cooler, and how to enjoy special INDIAN SUMMER days and nights. Consider some of these ways to bring you closer at this time of year:

1ST DAY OF FALL - SEPTEMBER

ACTIVITIES

1- Place AUTUMN theme stickers on your face or body for your Honey to discover

2- Play or sing *AUTUMN LEAVES* or *WHEN I FALL IN LOVE*, and dance together

3- Make love in a sleeping bag on this AUTUMN night - on the deck or in the back yard

4- Write notes about "FALLING" for your Sweetie – leave them in special places

5- Walk in the woods to look at the LEAVES - bring a blanket

6- Use AUTUMN colored sheets and pillowcases

7- Leave a trail of ACORNS or LEAVES in house or apartment - leading to you

8- Share a list of fun things to do outside together - this FALL

9- Wear RAIN HAT or GLOVES to bed - remove when the fun begins

10- FALL out of bed and ask your Partner to kiss wherever it hurts

GIFTS

1- Mug filled with PUMPKIN SEEDS or NUTS

2- Blanket – to look at LEAVES in the woods

3- SQUIRREL - ceramic, plastic or stuffed toy

4- PUMPKIN shaped sponge

5- T-shirt or nightshirt in ORANGE, GOLD or with an AUTUMN theme

FOOD

1- Toast the season with MULLED wine or spiced APPLE CIDER

2- Prepare a meal with LEAF shaped pasta

3- Serve a special AUTUMN breakfast, lunch, dinner or dessert

4- Share a large PUMPKIN or SWEET POTATO pie

5- Create a HEARTY soup together

♥

WINTER

The "1ST DAY OF WINTER" can be a special occasion. More time is spent inside as the weather cools, and in some places winter means snow. Here are some ideas to make the "1ST DAY OF WINTER" memorable:

1ST DAY OF WINTER – DECEMBER

ACTIVITIES

1-   Use solid WHITE sheets and pillowcases

2-   Run out into the COLD air on the deck or in the yard, wearing only underwear or nothing at all

3-   Buy a SNOWMAN or SNOWFLAKE sponge for bathing or showering together

4-   Play or sing WINTER WONDERLAND, LET IT SNOW or BABY IT'S COLD OUTSIDE, and dance together

5-   Place SNOWFLAKE stickers on your face or body where your Honey will discover them

6-   Write funny or suggestive phrases for ways to stay WARM - leave them where he or she will find them

7-   Wear a KNIT HAT or EARMUFFS to bed - remove when the laughter stops

8-   Share a list of outdoor activities you would like to do with your Honey this WINTER

9-   Make love in front of a ROARING FIRE

10-   Plan a WINTER weekend or a vacation get-a-way

♥

GIFTS

1- WHITE silk boxers for him or her

2- Cinnamon sticks for HOT chocolate, HOT tea or HOT toddies

3- WHITE scented candles for the bedroom

4- HOT chocolate and WHITE MARSHMALLOWS

5- WHITE candy - attached to a toy snow shovel, miniature boots or sled

FOOD

1- Serve a special WINTER breakfast, lunch, dinner or dessert

2- Enjoy an aerosol can of WHITE whipped cream

3- Share dessert, a cocktail or hot chocolate while watching the SNOW fall

4- Make soup with CHICKEN shaped pasta

5- Create a platter of special goodies – to enjoy in front of a ROARING FIRE

HOLIDAYS

Most of the major holidays are listed on the following pages. Remember you can celebrate any holiday – major or minor. Look through calendars to find some out of the ordinary annual listings. Some examples: Bastille Day, the birthday of your favorite artist, Groundhog Day or Earth Day.

HOLIDAY LIST

New Year's Day - January*

Groundhog Day - February

Valentine's Day - February*

Mardi Gras - February

Presidents' Day - February

St. Patrick's Day - March*

Easter - March/April

Passover - March/April

April Fool's Day

Secretaries' Day - April

May Day

Teacher Appreciation Day

Mothers' Day - May

Memorial Day – May*

Flag Day - June *

Fathers' Day - June

4th of July*

Bastille Day - July

Labor Day - September

Rosh Hashanah - September/October

Columbus Day - October*

Halloween - October*

Election Day - November

Veterans' Day - November

Thanksgiving - November*

Christmas - December

Hanukkah - November/December

New Year's Eve/New Year's Day*

*These holidays can be found in the following pages with creative ideas for activities, gifts and food.

♥

NEW YEAR'S EVE/NEW YEAR'S DAY

ACTIVITIES

1-   Model your GOLD or SILVER underwear

2-   Use a CHAMPAGNE bottle to pour juice, water or milk

3-   Write "HAPPY NEW YEAR" on your body where it will be found - use washable markers

4-   Share a list of NEW YEAR'S resolutions for you to do together in the coming year

5-   Place HAPPY NEW YEAR or CHAMPAGNE bottle stickers on your face or body for your Sweetie to discover

6-   Bathe together using CHAMPAGNE bubble bath

7-   Wear a NEW YEAR'S EVE hat to bed - remove when laughter stops

8-   Make love in a NEW place or in a NEW way

9-   Surprise your Honey with HAPPY NEW YEAR pillowcases

10-   Celebrate with GOLD or SILVER candles in the bedroom

♥

GIFTS

1-   GOLD, SILVER or HAPPY NEW YEAR pillowcases

2-   GOLD, SILVER or HAPPY NEW YEAR silk boxers
      - for him or her

3-   Nuts, candy, or scarf in CHAMPAGNE bottle

4-   HAPPY NEW YEAR t-shirt or nightshirt

5-   Bubble bath in CHAMPAGNE bottle

FOOD

1-   Create a meal with CHARDONNAY flavored pasta

2-   Prepare a special NEW YEAR'S breakfast, lunch,
      dinner or dessert

3-   Have breakfast in bed on NEW YEAR'S DAY

4-   Mix CHAMPAGNE with morning or afternoon fruit
      juice

5-   Serve CHAMPAGNE with lunch or dinner to toast the
      NEW YEAR

♥

VALENTINE'S DAY

ACTIVITIES

1-   Bathe or shower together using a HEART shaped sponge

2-   Wear RED underwear for your Partner to discover

3-   Make the bed with RED or WINE - colored sheets and pillowcases, or VALENTINE pillowcases

4-   Place VALENTINE stickers on your face or body where your Honey will find them

5-   Write loving/suggestive phrases on RED or PINK paper, and stick them on doors, walls, cabinets, or mirrors

6-   Play ROMANTIC music when he or she returns from work or an errand

7-   Tie a RED ribbon around neck, waist or other body parts

8-   Apply CHOCOLATE body paint

9-   Find VALENTINE toilet paper

10-   Model a RED apron with almost nothing or nothing underneath - man or woman

GIFTS

1-   RED elbow pads or knee pads for your Honey

2-   CD of favorite LOVE songs

3-   VALENTINE mug filled with red candy kisses

4-   RED underwear for him/ RED undies or teddy for her

5-   Anything CHOCOLATE, RED or with a
      VALENTINE   print

FOOD

1-   Enjoy a snack, dinner, dessert or a cocktail in front of
      a ROARING FIRE

2-   Serve HEART shaped pasta

3-   Dine at a ROMANTIC restaurant

4-   Create a special VALENTINE breakfast, lunch,
      dinner or dessert

5-   Use RED or VALENTINE napkins

♥

ST. PATRICK'S DAY

You don't have to be IRISH to have fun on this day!

ACTIVITIES

1-   Use SHAMROCK stickers on your face or body for your Honey to discover

2-   Bathe or shower together using a SHAMROCK sponge

3-   Play IRISH music when your Sweetie comes home from work or an errand

4-   Buy SHAMROCK toilet paper

5-   Let your Partner know that you are LUCKY to have him or her in your life

6-   Give or send a ST. PATRICK'S DAY card

7-   Model a GREEN or SHAMROCK apron with almost nothing underneath

8-   Tell your Honey that he or she will get LUCKY tonight

9-   Write funny/suggestive messages on GREEN or SHAMROCK paper and stick them on walls, doors or mirrors

10-   Wear GREEN underwear for him or her to discover

GIFTS

1- GREEN or SHAMROCK mug filled with green and white candy

2- SHAMROCK sponge

3- GREEN underwear for him/ GREEN undies or teddy for her

4- SHAMROCK pillowcases

5- Small POT OF GOLD for coins, paper clips or candy

FOOD

1- Prepare SHAMROCK shaped pasta

2- Use GREEN or SHAMROCK print napkins

3- Eat at an IRISH PUB

4- Plan a special IRISH or GREEN breakfast, lunch, dinner or dessert

5- Buy GREEN cookies, muffins, bagels or IRISH soda bread

♥

MEMORIAL DAY
FLAG DAY AND 4ᵀᴴ OF JULY

ACTIVITIES

1-   Wear STARS and STRIPES apron with almost nothing underneath – man or woman

2-   Show your Honey how to create FIREWORKS in the bedroom

3-   Hide a special or funny FLAG card in the refrigerator, microwave, or cabinet

4-   Use RED, WHITE and BLUE pillowcases

5-   Place FLAG stickers on your face or body where your Sweetie will discover them

6-   Model t-shirt or nightshirt with STARS and STRIPES print

7-   Stick small FLAGS in plants, toilet paper, computer keyboard or car for your Partner to discover

8-   Bathe or shower together with FLAG sponge or FLAG washcloth

9-   Leave a trail of small FLAGS on the floor - leading to you

10-   Buy STARS and STRIPES toilet paper

♥

GIFTS

1-   STARS and STRIPES/ FLAG beach towel

2-   STARS and STRIPES theme scarf, t-shirt, sport sox or tie.

3-   Candy that POPS/ EXPLODES in your mouth

4-   STARS and STRIPES apron

5-   Athletic cup or lace undies filled with RED, WHITE and BLUE jelly beans

FOOD

1-   Create a meal with FLAG & STAR shaped pasta

2-   Use STARS and STRIPES napkins, paper plates and paper cups

3-   Serve a special PATRIOTIC breakfast, lunch, dinner or dessert

4-   Stick small FLAGS in food

5-   Eat ice cream with RED, WHITE and BLUE sprinkles or with strawberries and blueberries - off of your Honey's stomach

♥

COLUMBUS DAY

You don't have to be Italian to have fun on this day!

ACTIVITIES

1-   Play or sing ITALIAN songs and dance together

2-   Share a bottle of WINE while bathing together

3-   List the reasons why your Honey is the best person in the WORLD for you and share them with him or her

4-   Go to a COLUMBUS DAY parade together

5-   Wear RED, WHITE and GREEN, or GLOBE print silk boxers – man or woman

6-   Give or send a special card – implying he or she is the best thing in your WORLD

7-   Suggest the two of you do some EXPLORING

8-   Buy a t-shirt or nightshirt with ITALIAN theme

9-   Place a tiny GLOBE under your Partner's pillow

10-   Write " WORLDLY" phrases - you mean the WORLD to me, welcome to my WORLD, share my WORLD and stick on doors, walls, cabinets or mirrors

GIFTS

1- GLOBE for desk or office

2- Bottle of WINE or SPARKLING JUICE

3- GLOBE yo-yo

4- Candle in an empty WINE bottle

5- CD of ITALIAN songs

FOOD

1- Enjoy a special ITALIAN lunch, dinner or dessert

2- Play ITALIAN music during lunch, dinner or dessert

3- Drink red WINE with lunch or dinner

4- Eat at an ITALIAN restaurant this day every year

5- Sprinkle HOT PEPPER on your dinner

♥

HALLOWEEN

ACTIVITIES

1-   Use BLACK or ORANGE sheets and pillowcases

2-   Have your Honey find you in an ORANGE, BLACK or HALLOWEEN print apron with almost nothing or nothing underneath - man or woman

3-   Buy HALLOWEEN theme toilet paper

4-   Place HALLOWEEN stickers on your face or body for your Sweetie to discover

5-   Wear a MASK to bed - remove after the laughter stops

6-   Dress in COSTUME together to greet trick or treaters

7-   Host a HALLOWEEN costume party or go to one

8-   Model BLACK or ORANGE underwear for your Partner

9-   Hide a HALLOWEEN card in the kitchen, bathroom or bedroom

10-   Leave a trail of CANDY in house or apartment - leading to you

GIFTS

1-   BLACK or ORANGE candles

2-   Book or magazine on CARVING PUMPKINS

3-   BAT or PUMPKIN shaped sponge for showering or bathing together

4-   Plastic PUMPKIN filled with candy, gum and apples

5-   BLACK knee pads for your Honey

FOOD

1-   Prepare PUMPKIN shaped pasta

2-   Use BLACK or ORANGE napkins

3-   Arrange a special HALLOWEEN brunch, lunch, dinner or dessert

4-   Buy BLACK and ORANGE candy

5-   Eat breakfast, lunch or dinner in COSTUME or with a MASK

♥

THANKSGIVING

ACTIVITIES

1-   Make a list of reasons why you are THANKFUL that your Honey is in your life and read them together

2-   Buy a mug with a THANKSGIVING or TURKEY theme

3-   Wear a PILGRIM hat or INDIAN headband with feather to bed – remove when the fun begins

4-   Hide a THANKSGIVING card in the refrigerator, microwave, cabinet or closet

5-   Place THANKSGIVING stickers on your face or body where your Partner will discover them

6-   Find THANKSGIVING theme toilet paper

7-   Bathe or shower together using a TURKEY shaped sponge

8-   THANK him or her when making love

9-   Model a THANKSGIVING theme apron with little or nothing underneath - man or woman

10-   Use PUMPKIN color sheets and pillowcases

GIFTS

1- Chocolate TURKEY

2- Silk boxers with a THANKSGIVING print for him or her

3- PUMPKIN color bath towel

4- T-shirt or nightshirt with a TURKEY on the front or back

5- TURKEY - ceramic, soft toy or pillow

FOOD

1- Serve a special THANKSGIVING breakfast, lunch, dinner or dessert

2- Find TURKEY shaped pasta for soup or entree

3- THANKSGIVING dinner reservation at your Honey's favorite restaurant

4- Use TURKEY print napkins

5- Buy or make a PUMPKIN pie

♥

TRADITIONS OF LOVE AND LAUGHTER

You can start traditions by celebrating special occasions or holidays in certain ways, and you can change them at any time. Colors, messages or pictures on items should be different – according to "what" you are celebrating. Consider the following ideas:

TRADITIONS OF
LOVE AND LAUGHTER

Give coffee or tea MUGS

Model or buy SILK BOXERS - for him or her

Use WASHABLE MARKERS on your body

Send, give or hide greeting CARDS

Buy or wear colorful UNDERWEAR

Hang BANNERS in house or apartment

Place STICKERS on your body

Prepare special types of PASTA

Play appropriate MUSIC and DANCE together

Share T-SHIRTS or NIGHTSHIRTS

Find special SPONGES

Dress in FUNNY CLOTHES

♥

Wear funny CAPS or HATS to bed

Find theme NAPKINS and PAPER PLATES

Serve BREAKFAST in bed

Buy TOILET PAPER that reflects the occasion

Play special songs or leave messages on VOICE MAIL

Use CANDLES

Model or buy APRONS - for him or her

Place various types of CANDY or SMALL GIFTS – in
unexpected containers

Sleep on appropriate SHEETS and/ or PILLOWCASES

Purchase any kind of GIFT

Make LOVE in a special place or in a special way

Arrange a unique BREAKFAST, LUNCH, DINNER or
DESSERT

♥

EPILOGUE

Now that I have given you some ideas on how to laugh and show love, you're likely to be more creative in this area. Laughter can create intimacy and elevate the soul. Hopefully you'll look at life a little differently, and find more joy in your relationship.

We all have a playful side; we just need to show it more. You're only as old as the games you play. You can always "add more love and laughter" to your relationship and to your life!

ABOUT THE AUTHOR

Joyce Karchmar like each of us, has been on her own journey of discovery. She believes we are never too old to be young at heart and that laughter enhances intimacy. Laughter really is the best medicine. Her love and enjoyment of people is reflected in her work.

39097500R00056

Made in the USA
Middletown, DE
04 January 2017